Classic Style

60 Jewelry Designs to Make and Wear

Fresh Look

Classic Style

60
Jewelry Designs to Make and Wear

Fresh Look

Irina Miech

KALMBACH BOOKS

Kalmbach Books
21027 Crossroads Circle
Waukesha, Wisconsin 53186
www.Kalmbach.com/Books

Photography © Kalmbach Books 2012

Published in 2012
16 15 14 13 12   1 2 3 4 5

Manufactured in the United States of America

ISBN: 978-0-87116-457-5

Editor: *Karin Van Voorhees*
Art Director: *Lisa Bergman*
Illustrator: *Kellie Jaeger*
Photographer: *William Zuback, Jim Forbes*

Library of Congress Cataloging-in-Publication Data
Miech, Irina.
  Classic style, fresh look : 60 jewelry designs to make and wear / Irina Miech.
    p. : col. ill. ; cm.
  ISBN: 978-0-87116-457-5

  1. Jewelry making–Handbooks, manuals, etc. 2. Beadwork–Handbooks, manuals, etc. 3. Beadwork–Patterns. I. Title.
TT860 .M543 2012
745.594/2

Contents

Introduction

The art of jewelry design has flourished for centuries. Over time, many popular designs have become classic styles. Because of their familiarity and their rich history, they are often worn for special occasions such as weddings and other formal events. These classic styles are a wonderful influence for any jewelry designer, and the elements of these designs can be used to create your own contemporary classics.

In this book, I explore these classics and create new classic-inspired designs as well. I use traditional materials including pearls, crystals, and stones, and traditional design elements such as symmetry and repetition, as well as classic metals, focusing on gold and silver tones.

I've designed a fresh look variation for each classic look. These reflect current trends, and often they can be more casual in their style. Changing the look of each project was a wonderful design challenge. To reinterpret each design and create the fresh look, I've added mixed metals and asymmetrical design elements, changed nonmetal materials to metal materials, and added unusual design touches to give an element of surprise. I've used the classic look technique, often incorporating techniques borrowed from other projects and mixing them for new design possibilities.

As our modern lifestyles have changed, so has our attitude toward styles and trends, and even our new greener attitude has changed the way we think about the materials we use. I've used recycled materials, such as the recycled paper beads in the South Seas necklace variation. I've also given some variations a steampunk element, such as the gears in the Stacked Solitaire ring variation. By reinterpreting the classic looks and using contemporary trends, I've taken their traditional look and given each piece a new and inventive fresh look.

The jewelry-construction techniques taught in the projects are the building blocks of design that every beginning jewelry designer needs. My goal is to show how adaptable these techniques are and how you can not just learn them, but make them your own. All of these designs are open to limitless interpretation; each classic look and its fresh look variation shows how you can take one design and transform it with your own personal design aesthetic to create very different looks. They demonstrate the breadth of each technique and how to put together your own style in your own way.

In addition to being within the project directions, basic techniques are explained in greater detail beginning on page 107.

Thanks for joining me in this creative journey!

Anna Miech

Projects

Dewdrop
necklace

Fresh
LOOK

The easiest way to shift from traditional to contemporary is to add playful metal elements. The warm tones and hammered textures of Patricia Healey's handmade findings are an interesting variation on the delicate crystal look. The vibrant colors of the torch-created patina work well with copper jump rings and dark Swarovski crystals to create an energetic and swirling design.

materials

- 13mm briolette
- **4** 11mm briolettes
- **2–4** 9mm briolettes
- **2** 7mm briolettes
- **55** 4mm Swarovski bicone crystals
- **54** 4mm Swarovski round crystals
- 15º seed beads
- 24-gauge headpin
- **2** crimp tubes
- 2-in. (5cm) large-link extender chain
- **2** 24-in. (61cm) lengths of .010 flexible beading wire
- Lobster claw clasp

tools

- Roundnose pliers
- Chainnose pliers
- Crimping pliers
- Side cutters
- Flexible beading wire cutters

a

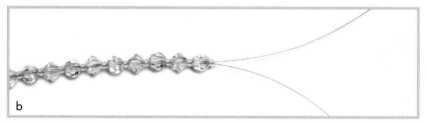

b

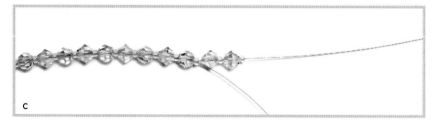

c

d

1 Crimp both lengths of the beading wire to the clasp (see page 109 for a closer look at crimping two wires together).

2 String round and bicone crystals over both wires (treating them as one), alternating with 15º seed beads, for 6 in. (15cm). End with a 15º **(a, b)**.

3 Separate the strands. One strand will be referred to as the top strand, and one strand will be referred to as the bottom strand. String a bicone, a 15º, a bicone, and a 15º on the top strand **(c)**.

4 String a round crystal, a 7mm briolette, and a round crystal on the bottom strand **(d)**.

f

e

g

5 String the bottom strand through the last 15º of the top strand in the opposite direction so that the 15º sits sideways between the two rows as shown **(e)**. The top strand will now be the bottom strand and the bottom strand will now be the top strand.

6 Repeat steps 3–5, but for the 7mm briolette make the following substitutions: 9mm briolettes (once or twice), 11mm briolettes (twice), a 13mm briolette (once), 11mm briolettes (twice), 9mm briolettes (once or twice), and a 7mm briolette (once) (this time stringing through the 15º in the same direction) **(f)**.

7 Over both strands, string round and bicone crystals, alternating with 15ºs, for 6 in.

8 Crimp both strands to the extender chain. String a bicone crystal onto a headpin and attach it to the extender chain with a wrapped loop **(g)**.

More About the Fresh Look

I had a lot of fun constructing this chain. Washers by Patricia Healey were my starting place, because they reflected the warm copper tones in the cones and spiral connectors. Linking the washers with double sets of jump rings added texture. A few beaded crystal links extended the chain and gave the subtle flash I wanted.

A Key to My Heart
necklace

CLASSIC Style

For this sparkling, delicate design, I used rhinestone components and crystals to achieve a lightweight, classic look.

Fresh
LOOK

For the other side of
the coin, I designed
an earthier, muted
palette, using
leather cord and
mixing different
colors of metals
to create a casual,
steampunk-inspired
look. The key motif
anchors both
designs, but with
very different effects.

materials

- **17** 4mm Swarovski rondelle crystals
- **12** 4mm rhinestone rondelle beads
- Charlottes
- Rhinestone multihole diamond component
- Rhinestone key charm
- **3** 4mm jump rings
- **3** 1½ in. (3.8cm) 24-gauge sterling silver headpins
- 2-in. (5cm) large-link extender chain
- **2** crimp tubes
- 20–24 in. (51–61cm) flexible beading wire
- Rhinestone clasp

tools

- Roundnose pliers
- Chainnose pliers
- Flatnose pliers
- Crimping pliers
- Side cutters
- Flexible beading wire cutters

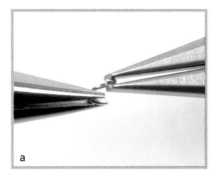

a

b

c

d

e

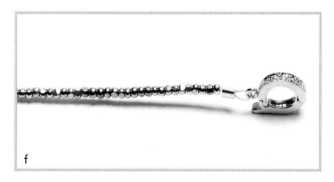

f

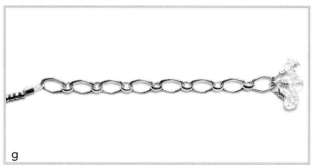

g

1 Using chainnose and flatnose pliers, open a jump ring **(a)**.

2 Slide the jump ring through two of the openings of the rhinestone multihold diamond component as shown **(b)** and close the jump ring.

3 Use two jump rings to connect the key charm to the jump ring from step 2 **(c)**.

4 String the flexible beading wire through two of the openings on the diamond component opposite the jump ring **(d)**.

5 On each end, string a charlotte. String an alternating pattern of seven crystal rondelles and six rhinestone rondelle beads. String 7–8 in. (18–20cm) of charlottes **(e)**.

6 String a crimp bead and a clasp loop. Go back through the crimp bead. Crimp the crimp bead with crimping pliers. Trim the excess beading wire **(f)**.

7 On the other end, repeat step 6, but crimp the wire to the extender chain.

8 String a crystal rondelle onto a headpin and attach it to the end of the extender chain with a wrapped loop. Repeat twice **(g)**.

Floating Jade
necklace

CLASSIC Style

Jade beads are a very traditional material, and the three-strand design uses SilverSilk chain to create a streamlined look.

Fresh
LOOK

Mixed metal chains in different styles provide a fun twist. Layering the metal chains creates a fluid effect and is reminiscent of the lines created with the ethnic components in the first design, but has more movement.

materials

- **18–20** assorted large-hole jade beads
- **2** 9mm twisted jump rings
- **8** 5mm jump rings
- **2** 3-in. (7.6cm) chain lengths
- **30–36** crimp tubes
- **30–36** crimp covers
- **2** pinch ends with prongs (3mm interior diameter)
- 6 in. (15cm) 28-gauge craft wire
- **3** 14-in. (36cm) lengths of SilverSilk three-needle chain
- Hook-and-loop clasp

tools

- Flatnose pliers
- Crimping pliers
- Side cutters

a

b

c

d

e

f

1 String a wire through all three pieces of three-needle chain approximately 4mm from the end **(a)**.

2 Wrap the wire tightly around the ends of the three-needle chain **(b)**. Cut and tuck in the ends of the wire **(c, d)**.

3 Insert the bundled ends of the three-needle chain into the pinch end as far as it will go (you may need to open the pinch end slightly wider than it already is using flatnose pliers) **(e)**. Use flatnose pliers to firmly close the pinch end **(f)**.

4 Use flatnose pliers to slightly reduce the diameter of the three-needle chain by pinching it **(g)**. String a crimp tube onto one of the lengths of the three-needle chain approximately 1–1½ in. (2.5–3.8cm) from the end, and crimp it with crimping pliers **(h, i)**.

5 Put a crimp cover over the crimp and use flatnose pliers to close it **(j)**.

6 String a bead and another crimp tube onto the same length of the chain. Crimp and cover the crimp **(k)**.

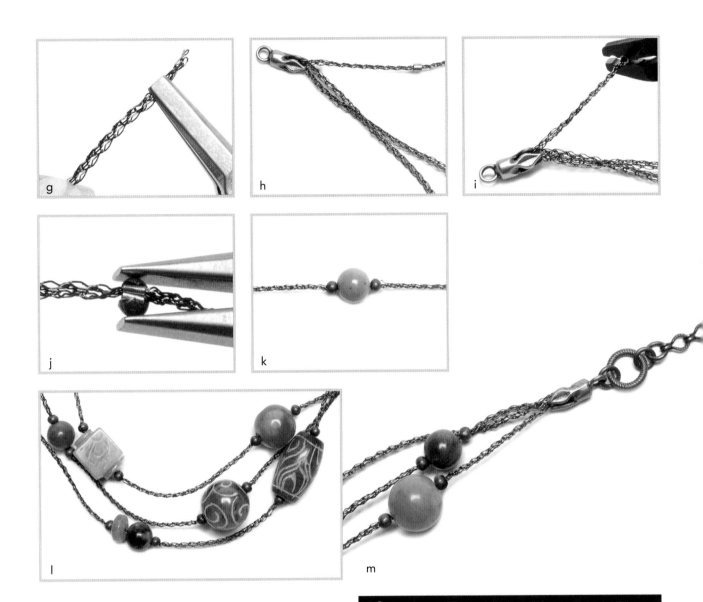

g

h

i

j

k

l

m

7 Continue adding beads or groups of beads in this manner, always placing a crimp and crimp cover on each side, and spacing the beads 1½–2 in. (3.8–5cm) apart **(l)**.

8 Bead the remaining two lengths of the three-needle chain similarly, staggering the beads relative to the other chains.

9 Repeat steps 1–3 on the other end.

10 Attach a jump ring to the connecting loop of the pinch end, then a textured jump ring, and two more jump rings. Attach a chain length to the last jump ring **(m)**.

11 Repeat step 10 on the other end.

12 Use jump rings to connect a hook to one end of the necklace and a loop to the other end.

More About the Fresh Look

Chain is a strong jewelry-design component, and today, there are more varieties than ever available. Finishes like gunmetal, brass, and copper make it an affordable choice as well. It's fun to layer different styles. In this piece, I combined rollo, cable, modified figure-8, ball and bar, and the same silver silk used in the Classic Style necklace.

South Seas
necklace

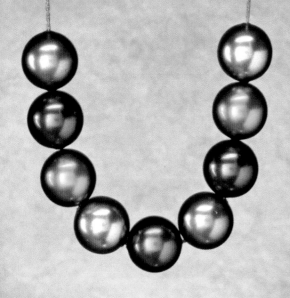

CLASSIC Style

Tahitian pearls are a gorgeous, classic element of jewelry design, and these perfectly round shell pearls echo their look and color. The delicate beading chain adds a minimalist, elegant touch.

Fresh LOOK

For the variation, chunky recycled paper beads give the necklace an ethnic look and are very earth-friendly. Using green materials is a great way to give a classic design a new look. I also added mixed metals and double bead caps for a modern touch.

materials

- **10** 10mm shell pearls
- **2** 5mm jump rings
- Headpin
- **2** crimp loop findings
- 16–18 in. (41–46cm) beading chain
- 2-in. (5cm) large-link extender chain
- Hook clasp

tools

- Roundnose pliers
- Flatnose pliers
- Side cutters

More About the Fresh Look

These paper beads are from the Akonye Kena Self-Sufficiency Project Ltd. Akonye Kena means "I will help myself" in Acholi, a northern Ugandan tribal language. The program provides artisans in Uganda a venue to sell their goods and earn a sustainable income. The organization was founded in 2009 by Richard Kennair.

1 Insert the end of the beading chain into a crimp loop finding **(a)**.

2 Use flatnose pliers to crimp the crimp loop finding **(b)**.

3 String the pearls onto the beading chain in an aesthetically pleasing order **(c)**.

4 Repeat steps 1 and 2 on the other chain end.

5 Attach a hook to one end loop with a jump ring **(d)**.

6 Attach an extender chain to the other end loop with a jump ring.

7 String a pearl on a headpin and attach it to the end of the extender chain with a wrapped loop **(e)**.

Filigree
Chandelier
earrings

CLASSIC Style

I have always liked the elegant look of Victorian jewelry, and these rhinestone filigree earrings evoke that classic era.

Fresh LOOK

For a fresh spin, I thought of my travels to French Polynesia and looked to traditional Polynesian patterns. I chose carved shell components and complemented them with pearls in a lighter color. The subtle shimmer and organic feel of the shell components is in contrast to the elegant, formal look of the rhinestone earrings.

materials

NOTE: All crystals are Swarovski Elements.

- **2** 6mm round crystals
- **6** 4mm rondelle crystals
- **2** 4mm rhinestone rondelle beads
- **12** 3mm bicone crystals
- **12** 3mm daisy spacers
- **6** 1½- or 2-in. (3.8 or 5cm) 24-gauge headpins
- **2** filigree chandelier earring components
- Pair of rhinestone earring wires

tools

- Roundnose pliers
- Chainnose pliers
- Side cutters

a

b

1 On a headpin, string: a 3mm bicone crystal, a daisy spacer, a 6mm round crystal, a rhinestone rondelle, a 4mm crystal rondelle, a daisy spacer, and a 3mm bicone crystal **(a)**.

2 Make a wrapped loop, attaching the headpin component through the central loop on the filigree finding **(b)**. Complete the wraps **(c)** into the gap.

3 Trim the end of the headpin flush. Use chainnose pliers to tuck the wire end between the wraps and the bead.

c

d

e

4 String: a 3mm bicone crystal, a daisy spacer, a 4mm crystal rondelle, a daisy spacer, and a 3mm bicone crystal on a headpin. Repeat to make two dangles.

5 Repeat steps 2–3, attaching the dangles to the remaining loops of the filigree **(d)**.

6 Attach the earring wire to the top of the filigree finding **(e)**.

7 Make a second earring.

More About the Fresh Look

When using nontraditional components such as shell, the metal choice for findings might not seem obvious. Here, the gold picks up the warm tones of the shell and is echoed in the dangling accent crystals.

Crystal Romance
necklace & earrings

CLASSIC Style

Loops and jump rings are the building blocks of jewelry design, and the foundation for this set. With these simple techniques, you can design a wide range of pieces. Even the same design can have an entirely different look if you simply change the elements. Sparkling crystals and bright metals distinguish the classic version.

Fresh
LOOK

Nontraditional metals, steampunk-inspired components, and a touch of Victorian whimsy in the use of the bee charm mark the variation. Both designs use the same foundation—loops and jump rings—but the resulting jewelry is entirely unique.

25

materials

necklace
- 8mm crystal ball
- 20mm Swarovski crystal ring
- **4** 6mm Swarovski round crystals
- 1½ in. (3.8cm) 24-gauge headpin
- **3** 8mm jump rings
- **2** 4mm jump rings
- **5** 3mm jump ring
- 2-in. (5cm) large-link extender chain
- **2** 9-in. (23cm) pieces medium-link chain
- ⅜-in. (1cm) piece fine-link chain
- 22-gauge wire
- Hook clasp

earrings
- **2** 8mm crystal balls
- **6** 6mm Swarovski round crystals
- **2** ⅜-in. (1cm) pieces fine-link chain
- 22-gauge wire
- Pair of earring wires

tools
- Roundnose pliers
- Chainnose pliers
- Flatnose pliers
- Side cutters

a

b

c   d

e

f

earrings

1 Make a wrapped loop at the end of the wire. String a 6mm crystal onto the wire and make a wrapped loop at the other end of the wire **(a–c)**.

2 Repeat step 1 to make nine wrapped loop/crystal components. Set three aside for the necklace.

3 Use 3mm jump rings to connect three of the loop/crystal components **(d)**.

4 Use a 3mm jump ring to connect this grouping to one of the lengths of fine-link chain. Use another jump ring to connect the other end of the chain piece to the crystal ball **(e)**.

5 Use chainnose pliers to attach the earring wire **(f)**.

6 Make a second earring.

g

h

necklace

7 Repeat steps 3 and 4 using the remaining wrapped-loop/crystal components.

8 Use an 8mm jump ring to attach a crystal ring and use two more 8mm jump rings to attach the two pieces of medium-link chain **(g)**.

9 Use a 4mm jump ring to attach the hook clasp. Use a 4mm jump ring to attach the large-link extender chain. String a 6mm crystal on a headpin and attach it to the end of the extender chain with a wrapped loop **(h)**.

More About the Fresh Look

Gear components as well as other rings can be converted into connector components with the simple addition of jump rings.

Elegant
Three-Strand
necklace & earrings

CLASSIC Style

It doesn't get more classic than a three-strand necklace of graduated pearls subtly sprinkled with Swarovski crystals and finished with an elegant sterling silver CZ multistrand clasp.

Fresh LOOK

Metal components, color blocking, and varying the shapes and textures of beads bring a fresh, up-to-the minute feel to this design.

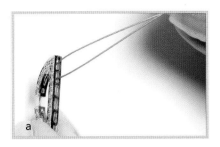

a

b

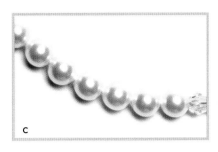

c

d

e

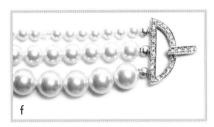

f

materials

necklace

- 8mm white glass pearls
- 6mm white glass pearls
- 4mm white glass pearls
- 6mm Swarovski round crystals
- 4mm Swarovski round crystals
- 3mm Swarovski bicone crystals
- **6** crimp beads
- **6** crimp covers
- Flexible beading wire
- Multistrand rhinestone clasp

earrings

- **2** 8mm glass pearls
- **2** rhinestone bead caps
- **2** headpins
- Pair of rhinestone earring wires

tools

- Roundnose pliers
- Chainnose pliers
- Crimping pliers
- Side cutters

necklace

1 Cut a 20-in. (51cm) piece of flexible beading wire and string the end through the top opening of the clasp; go around the small bar so the end of the flexible beading wire exits through the next opening **(a)**.

2 Crimp the flexible beading wire to the clasp **(b)**. Cover the crimp with a crimp cover.

3 String a pattern of seven 4mm glass pearls and a 3mm bicone crystal for 16 in. (41cm) **(c)**.

4 Repeat steps 1 and 2 on the other end.

5 Cut a 21-in. (53cm) length of beading wire. Repeat steps 1 and 2, but crimp to the middle clasp bar.

6 String a pattern of five 6mm glass pearls and a 4mm round crystal for 17 in. (43cm) **(d)**.

7 Repeat steps 1 and 2 to finish the other end of this strand (remember to crimp to the corresponding bar).

8 Cut a 22-in. (56cm) piece of beading wire. Repeat steps 1 and 2, but crimp to the remaining clasp bar.

9 String a pattern of seven 6mm glass pearls and a 6mm round crystal for 18 in. (46cm) **(e)**.

10 Repeat steps 1 and 2 on the other end of the strand (crimp to the corresponding bar) **(f)**.

earrings

11 String an 8mm glass pearl, a rhinestone cone, and a 3mm glass pearl on a headpin.

12 Make a wrapped loop, attaching the decorative earring wire. Make a second earring.

*
More About the Fresh Look

It was a little harder to maintain the graduated look of the original using different shapes of beads, but it was a fun challenge!

Endless Pearls
necklace

CLASSIC Style

The knotted pearl necklace is a very traditional design, developed so that if the strand broke, at the most only a single pearl would be lost. This necklace echoes that practice, and it has neither beginning nor end.

Fresh LOOK

Instead of stringing these beads onto the silk, I've used large textured jump rings to suspend them, which gives the design lots of movement and visual interest. There are flashes of jewel-like color, as well as a touch of romance and vintage, in the use of acrylic, lightweight flowers. The necklace is asymmetrical yet balanced, and the dragonfly and butterfly decoupage beads add an element of fun.

materials

- **11** 10mm shell pearls
- **28–30** 8mm shell pearls
- **10** 8mm round crystals
- **10** 5mm squaredelles
- Silk cord, size 6, with needle attached

tools and supplies

- Bead Stoppers
- G-S Hypo Cement
- Scissors

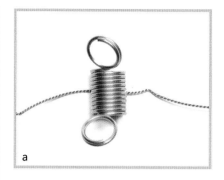

a

b

c

d

e

f

1 Secure a Bead Stopper or clamp approximately 5 in. (13cm) from the end of the cord opposite the needle **(a)**.

2 String a pearl onto the cord and slide it on until it rests against the clamp. Tie an overhand knot next to the pearl **(b–e)**.

3 Tie another knot approximately 1 in. (2.5cm) from the first knot. String a bead and tie another knot on the other side **(f)**.

4 Continue to add single beads and groupings of multiple beads until you have reached the desired length **(g)**.

5 To finish the necklace, tie a knot and string part of a grouping of beads on one end and, after removing the clamp, a single bead on the other **(h)**.

g

h

i

j

k

More About the Fresh Look

Visual weight is important in design, but you can keep your piece comfortable and wearable by using light-weight materials such as decoupage and acrylic beads.

6 Tie the two ends in a square knot (i).

7 Put a small amount of glue on the knot (j), and press the beads together. Let the glue set.

8 Once the glue is dry, cut off the excess cord (k).

Vintage
Filigree Blooms

CLASSIC Style

I have always liked the Art Nouveau movement. The filigree components in the necklace are reproductions of Art Nouveau designs and contain motifs from that time period—not just from jewelry but also from architecture and art. I thought it would be interesting to juxtapose these stylized flowers and butterflies, and contrast their shapes and colors to create a striking, substantial piece of jewelry.

Fresh LOOK

To create variation, I isolated a single element and added a bit of movement with an eclectic selection of charms and chain, as well as another flash of color. Bringing a kinetic aspect to this piece worked very well, and the resulting pendant can be worn for nearly any occasion.

a

b

c

materials

- **11** filigree components
- Filigree rings for stacking (optional)
- Rivolis and CZs (one per component unless the component is already set with a stone)
- 8mm bead with rhinestones
- headpin
- **14** 7mm jump rings
- 5 in. (13cm) chain
- hook clasp

tools and supplies

- Roundnose pliers
- Chainnose pliers
- Flatnose pliers
- Side cutters
- E6000 adhesive

1 Arrange the filigree components as you would like them to appear in the necklace. For the best impact, contrast shapes and colors of metal, and graduate the sizes of the components with the largest toward the front and the smaller elements toward the back.

2 Decide which of the filigree components are going to be stacked. Then pair rivolis and/or CZs with the corresponding filigree components, paying attention to size and color **(a)**.

3 Use the adhesive to adhere the metal components together and to set the rivolis/CZs **(b–f)**.

4 Let the components set for 24 hours.

d

e

f

g

h

i

More About the Fresh Look
This style lends itself nicely to personalization: Choose a birthstone color for the crystal dangle or flower center, or use a meaningful charm, a favorite orphan bead, or a non-jewelry object, such as a small key.

5 Use jump rings to connect all of the components **(g)**. Use any opening on the component as long as it's large enough to accommodate a jump ring. In order for the necklace to drape properly, use the openings on the upper half of the components as shown in the photo on page 34.

6 Cut the chain into a 1½- and a 3½-in. (3.8 and 8.9cm) piece. Attach one to each end of the necklace with jump rings.

7 Use a jump ring to attach a hook clasp to the shorter chain piece **(h)**. String a bead onto the headpin and attach it to the end of the longer piece of chain with a wrapped loop **(i)**.

Earth Elements
necklace

1 Use the Mighty Crimper to secure a crimp tube onto the leather cord approximately 1½ in. (3.8cm) from the center **(a)**.

2 Starting with a spacer bead, string an alternating pattern of eight spacers and seven gemstone beads. String them toward the longer side of the leather cord. Crimp a crimp tube on the other side of the grouping.

3 Crimp a crimp tube 2½–3 in. (6.4–7.6cm) from the last crimp and string another grouping of beads and spacers **(b)**.

CLASSIC Style

While this long necklace uses an unconventional stringing material, the groupings of gemstones and the delineated sets of color are traditional in style. The gemstones are center stage, while the stringing material plays a secondary role.

4 Keeping the first grouping in the center, continue to add groupings of beads and spacers on each end until you have seven groupings.

5 String a crimp tube and a hook clasp onto the cord approximately 2–3 in. (5–7.6cm) from the end, and string the cord back through the crimp (c). Use the Mighty Crimper to secure the crimp.

6 On the other end of the necklace, string a crimp tube and a ring onto the cord approximately 2–3 in. from the end, and string the cord back through the crimp tube. Use the Mighty Crimper to secure the crimp.

7 On one end, string a bead and a spacer. Tie an overhand knot and trim the excess cord. Repeat on the other end (d).

More About the Fresh Look

To finish the bracelet ends, I wrapped the leather cords into a bundle with 22-gauge wire, applied an adhesive (E6000), and pulled the end of the wire through the cap. I then made a wrapped loop with the wire tail to connect the clasp.

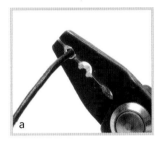
a

b

c

d

Fresh LOOK

Here, I shifted the focus away from the beads. I used different colors of leather cord, including metallic colors, bringing the cord out from the background and turning it into the main design element. The dangling pearls add a touch of movement and give the bracelet a fun and casual look. Because the pearls aren't fixed in place, they create an asymmetrical design that changes as the piece is worn.

Magic Rings
necklace & earrings

This necklace is inspired by the popular trend of large-hole beads. The great allure of these beads is that they are modular. You can wear them interchangeably, grouping them together in bands of color, or you can wear them one at a time.

Fresh
LOOK

This larger, bolder piece is created in a similar way, but instead of beading a single ring at a time, the whole piece is created at once as a very structured component. I added an element of color gradation and changed the color of the rings to a non-traditional metal. I used a Swarovski button at the base to give the piece a polished, finished look, and I added an Art Nouveau-style bee for a touch of fun.

materials

necklace
- **6** 10-hole round filigree components
- **31** 4mm Swarovski round crystals
  10 in two colors
  11 in one color
- **24**-gauge headpin
- **4** 6mm jump rings
- **2** pinch ends (3mm inside diameter)
- **3** 7-in. (18cm) lengths of 28-gauge craft wire
- **16** in. (41cm) SilverSilk capture chain
- **2**-in. (5cm) large-link extender chain
- Hook clasp

earrings
- **4** 10-hole round filigree components
- **20** 4mm Swarovski round crystals
- **2** 8mm jump rings
- **4** 6mm jump rings
- **2** 7-in. (18cm) lengths of 28-gauge craft wire
- **2** in. (5cm) fine-link chain
- Pair of earring wires

tools
- Roundnose pliers
- Chainnose pliers
- Flatnose pliers
- Side cutters

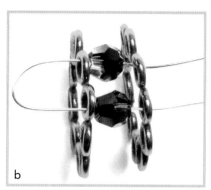

a

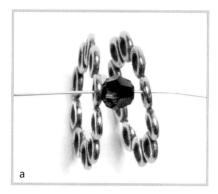

b

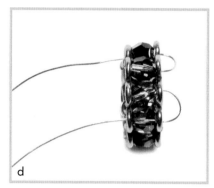

c

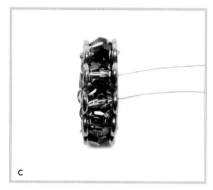

d

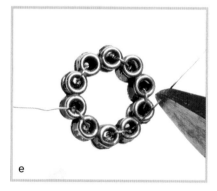

e

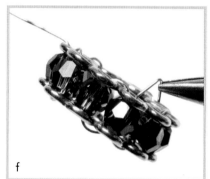

f

necklace

1 String a wire through a filigree component hole, a crystal, and a filigree component hole **(a)**.

2 String the wire end through an adjacent hole of the filigree component, a crystal, and the corresponding hole of a second filigree component **(b)**.

3 Continue to string the wire through all of the holes of both components, always adding a crystal between the components, until you have beaded between all of the holes **(c)**.

4 String through the adjacent beads with each wire end **(d)**, continuing in opposite directions until you have gone through at least two beads on each side of the intersection of the wire ends.

5 Cut the wire ends, leaving a 5mm tail **(e)**. Using chainnose pliers, bend the tail and tuck it into the hole of the next bead **(f, g)**.

6 Repeat steps 1–5 to make a total of three beaded rings.

g

h

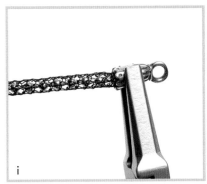

i

j

7 Insert the end of the capture chain into the pinch end as far as it will go **(h)**. Use flatnose pliers to firmly close the pinch end, first closing one pair of "petals" and then the other **(i)**.

8 Use a pair of jump rings to connect a hook clasp to one of the pinch ends. Use a jump ring to attach the extender chain to the other pinch end. String a 4mm Swarovski crystal onto a headpin and attach it to the extender chain with a wrapped loop **(j)**.

9 String the rings on the necklace. You can wear them together or separately.

earrings

10 Make a beaded ring as in steps 1–5 of the necklace.

11 Open an 8mm jump ring and string the beaded ring. Close the jump ring.

12 Open a 6mm jump ring and string the 8mm jump ring and the end link of chain. Close the jump ring.

13 Attach an earring wire to the other end of the chain.

14 Make a second earring.

✳ More About the Fresh Look

Color gradation is a visual experience. I like laying the crystals next to each other and seeing what works. Remember that a finish will alter the color and often will help you achieve a gradual color shift. Pay more attention to what the crystals look like than what they are named.

Flowering Dome
pendant & earrings

CLASSIC Style

The classic look is romantic, with clean lines and a touch of sparkle. The dome is a traditional design element, giving the piece a three-dimensional touch. The flower and the crystal teardrop are also traditional elements.

Fresh LOOK

To create something very different, I nested domes within each other, layering them with gears for a touch of steampunk. The leather gives the piece a more contemporary look, and the asymmetrical wire detail adds a little more metal for an urban feel.

materials

pendant

- 20mm textured metal disk
- Silver-tone flower charm
- 7x12mm Swarovski crystal drops
- Bail
- **3** 5mm jump rings
- 1-in. (2.5cm) piece of chain

earrings

- **2** 20mm textured metal disks
- **2** silver-tone flower charms
- **2** 7x12mm Swarovski crystal drops
- **4** 5mm jump rings
- **2** 1-in. (2.5cm) pieces of chain
- Pair of earring wires

tools

(both projects)

- Dapping block and punches
- Deadblow hammer
- Punch pliers
- Chainnose pliers
- Flatnose pliers
- Fine-tip marker

pendant

1 Place the disk texture-side down in a dapping block **(a)** and place a metal punch in the center of the disk. Strike the metal punch with a deadblow hammer multiple times until the disk is domed (use lighter strokes at first and dome the disk gradually) **(b)**.

2 Mark the placement of the two holes **(c)**, and use punch pliers to punch the holes **(d)**.

3 Open a jump ring with flatnose and chainnose pliers, and connect a crystal teardrop to the end of one of the pieces of chain **(e)**. Use a jump ring to connect the other end of the chain and a flower charm to the bottom hole of the domed disk **(f)**.

4 Use a jump ring to connect the bail to the top hole of the domed disk **(g)**.

earrings

5 Repeat steps 1–3 of the pendant.

6 Attach an earring wire to the hole at the top of the domed disk.

7 Make a second earring.

a

b

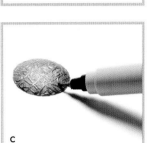

c

d

e

f

g

❋ More About the Fresh Look

There is a direct relationship between the size of the components and the degree of concavity. To achieve a nesting effect, dap the smaller pieces more than the larger disks.

Cleopatra's
collar

CLASSIC
Style

Sometimes a
component can
inspire a design. As
soon as I saw this
keystone-shaped
crystal, I immediately
thought of Cleopatra
and Egyptian designs.
I knew the crystal
shape would work
perfectly in a curved
necklace. I added
metal chain to give
the piece some
movement.

Fresh LOOK

For the variation, I used gunmetal instead of antiqued brass, which has become nearly a traditional metal in the past few years. Darker and bolder, gunmetal dramatically changes the look of the design. I also used two rows of keystone crystals to give this version more of a visual impact, and I changed the size and shape of the beads as well as the draping chain at the bottom of the piece for drama.

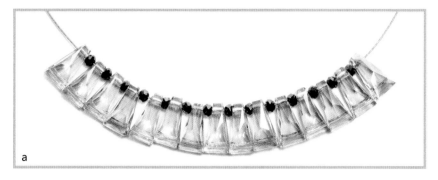

a

materials

necklace

NOTE: All metal components are antiqued brass.

- **15** 13mm Swarovski keystone crystals
- **17** 3mm rondelles
- **3** headpins
- **4** crimp tubes
- **4** crimp covers
- 40 in. (102cm) fine-link chain
- 4 in. (10cm) large-link chain
- 14 in. (36cm) flexible beading wire
- Hook clasp

earrings

- **2** 13mm Swarovski keystone crystals
- **2** eyepins
- **2** 7mm jump rings
- **2** 1½-in. (3.8cm) pieces of chain
- **2** 2½-in. (6.4cm) pieces of chain
- **2** earring wires

tools

(both projects)

- Roundnose pliers
- Chainnose pliers
- Flatnose pliers
- Crimping pliers
- Flexible beading wire cutters
- Side cutters

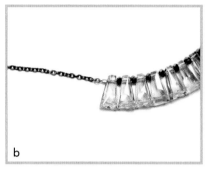

b

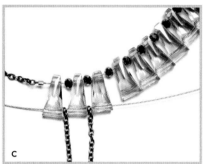

c

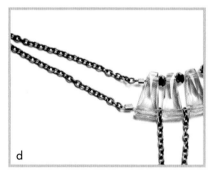

d

necklace

1 Cut the fine-link chain into seven 2½-in., two 5-in., and two 5⅛-in. (6.4, 13, and 13.1cm) pieces. Cut the large-link chain into a 3-in. and a 1-in. (7.6 and 2.5cm) piece. Cut the flexible beading wire into two 7-in. (18cm) pieces.

2 Use one piece of flexible beading wire to string the keystone crystals through the top hole, alternating them with 3mm rondelles **(a)**.

3 On each end, crimp the flexible beading wire to a 5-in. chain piece **(b)**.

4 On a piece of flexible beading wire, string the bottom hole of the first keystone crystal, one end link of a 2½-in. chain, the next keystone crystal, and the other end of the chain **(c)**.

Continue this pattern until you have used all of the pieces of chain and have strung through the last keystone crystal.

5 Crimp the flexible beading wire to a 5⅛-in. piece of chain on each end **(d)**.

6 Cover all four crimps with crimp covers **(e)**.

7 Open a jump ring and string it through both ends of the chain on one end of the necklace. Add the 1-in. large-link chain piece and close the jump ring. Use a jump ring to connect the hook clasp **(f)**.

e

f

g

h

i

j

k

8 Open a jump ring and string it through both ends of the chain on one side of the necklace. String the 3-in. piece of large-link chain and close the jump ring. String a 3mm rondelle on a headpin and attach to the end of the large-link chain with a wrapped loop. Repeat to make a total of three dangles **(g)**.

earrings

9 Open a jump ring and string it through the hole at the narrow side of the keystone crystal. String an earring wire onto the same jump ring and close it **(h)**.

10 Open an eyepin and string a 1½- (3.8cm) and a 2½-in. piece of chain. Close the loop **(i)**.

11 String the wide side of the keystone crystal on the eyepin **(j)**. Make a loop snug to the crystal and trim the excess wire **(k)**.

12 Open the loop, string both chain end links, and close the loop.

13 Make a second earring.

49

Moongate Pearl
necklace & earrings

CLASSIC Style

While vacationing in Bermuda, I was enchanted by moongates—simple circular gates made of stone, and a classic part of Bermudian architecture. The spacing of the rhinestones in these circular components reminded me of moongates. Here, two components and a pearl

Fresh LOOK

Similarly shaped but different in color, this pearl is paired with earthy river stones and textured jump rings. The juxtaposition of the high polish of the pearl against the matte finish of the river stones creates visual interest and a modern look.

a

b

c

d

e

f

g

materials

necklace
- 15mm round rhinestone multihole component
- 11mm round rhinestone multihole component
- 9x11mm half-drilled pearl
- rhinestone half-drilled pearl setting
- **2** 5mm jump rings
- **2** 4–6mm jump rings
- 16–18 in. (41–46cm) fine cable chain
- Lobster claw clasp

earrings
- **2** 15mm round rhinestone multihole components
- **2** 11mm round rhinestone multihole components
- **2** rhinestone half-drilled pearl settings
- **2** 9 x 11mm half-drilled pearls
- Pair of rhinestone earring wires

tools and supplies
- Chainnose pliers
- Flatnose pliers
- G-S Hypo Cement

necklace

1 Put a drop of glue on the prong of the pearl setting **(a)**. Insert it into the half-drilled pearl as far as it will go **(b)**. Let the glue set.

2 Open a jump ring and string through two of the openings on the side of the smaller rhinestone component as shown **(c)**.

3 String the pearl component onto the jump ring and close the jump ring **(d)**.

4 Open a jump ring and string through two openings of the same rhinestone component, opposite the first jump ring **(e)**.

5 String the jump ring through two of the openings on the side of the larger rhinestone component and close the jump ring **(f)**.

6 Slide the fine cable chain through two of the openings at the top of the pendant (opposite the jump ring) **(g)**. Use a jump ring to attach the clasp to one end of the chain. Attach a jump ring to the other end of the chain to complete the necklace.

earrings

7 Repeat necklace steps 1–5.

8 String a jump ring through two of the openings on the side of the larger rhinestone component opposite the first jump ring. String the earring wire through the jump ring and close the jump ring.

9 Make a second earring.

Pearl Nouveau
bracelet

CLASSIC Style

Art Nouveau is an iconic art movement from the turn of the century. One important element of many Art Nouveau pieces is symmetry. I used a reproduction of a filigree component from that time period as the main element. I mounted a pearl in the center, which is also a classic Art Nouveau material.

Fresh
LOOK

Here, the filigree component is incorporated in a nontraditional manner to frame a sparkling, very modern bead. I've added several pieces of chain in different styles and textures, and created an asymmetrical design.

materials

NOTE: All metal components are antiqued brass.

- **2** 6x8mm crystal rondelles
- 3x4mm crystal rondelle
- 6mm Swarovski pearl
- 21x64mm filigree component
- 17mm filigree ring
- **2** 10mm decorative rings
- **4** 9mm bead caps
- **2** eyepins
- Headpin
- **10** 9mm textured jump rings
- **9** 7mm jump rings
- 6 in. (15cm) 28-gauge craft wire
- 5x30mm toggle bar

tools

- Roundnose pliers
- Chainnose pliers
- Flatnose pliers
- Bracelet bending pliers
- 1.8mm hole-punching pliers
- Side cutters
- Fine-tip permanent marker

a

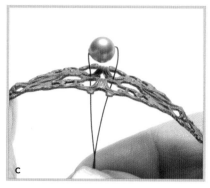

c

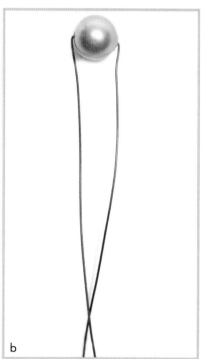

b

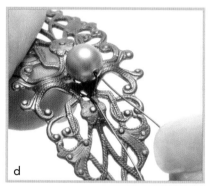

d

e

1 Use bracelet bending pliers to bend the filigree finding into a gentle curve **(a)**.

2 String the pearl on the wire and center it. Bend the wire down on both sides of the pearl **(b)**.

3 String each wire end through the center of the filigree **(c)**.

4 Cross a wire end under the pearl, come back up through an opening in the filigree, and go back through the pearl from the opposite side **(d)**. Repeat with the other wire end (at this point the wire will have passed through the pearl three times) **(e)**.

5 String the wire ends through the same openings to the back of the filigree component and secure each end by wrapping it two to three times around the set of wires on the back **(f)**.

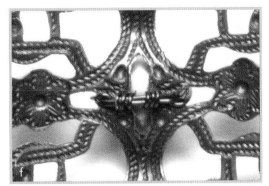

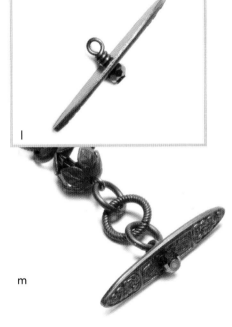

6 Mark the position of a hole at each end of the filigree component (g). Punch the holes with hole-punching pliers (h).

7 Connect a 7mm jump ring to one side of the filigree component. Connect a second jump ring to the first (i). Use two textured jump rings to connect a decorative ring. Connect two textured jump rings to the decorative ring. Connect a 7mm jump ring (j).

8 String a bead cap, an 8x6mm rondelle, and a bead cap onto a eyepin and make a loop at the end (k).

9 Connect the beaded link to the 7mm jump ring. Connect a 7mm jump ring to the other side of the beaded link.

10 Repeat steps 7–9 for the other side.

11 To make the toggle bar, string a 3x4mm crystal rondelle and a bar component onto a headpin. Make a wrapped loop (l).

12 Use a 7mm jump ring and a textured jump ring to connect the toggle bar to one side of the bracelet (m), and use a textured jump ring to connect the filigree ring to the other side of the bracelet (n).

More About the Fresh Look
The crystal teardrop inside the organically shaped filigree reminded me of a stylized calla lily.

Whimsical
Geometry
necklace & earrings

CLASSIC Style

Who knew that geometry could be so wearable? These sparkling shapes are a joy to create. The interlocking elements within each component are like tiny puzzles—so full of possibilities. They stack

Fresh LOOK

For the variation, I changed from a unified look to a mixed-metals look. I also used fewer geometric filigree components and added different links in contrasting metals to create a casual, fun style.

materials

necklace

- **16** filigree components in assorted shapes and sizes
- Assorted 2–5mm Swarovski crystal bicones and rounds
- Assorted 2–4mm pearls
- Assorted seed beads
- **32** 4mm jump rings
- 34 in. (86cm) chain
- 50–60 in. (1.3–1.5m) 28-gauge craft wire

earrings

- **2** filigree components
- Assorted 2–5mm Swarovski crystal bicones and rounds
- Assorted 2–4mm pearls
- Assorted seed beads
- **2** 24-gauge decorative headpins
- **6** 4mm jump rings
- **2** 2-link pieces of chain
- 5–10 in. (13–25cm) 28-gauge craft wire
- Pair of earring wires

tools

- Roundnose pliers
- Chainnose pliers
- Flatnose pliers
- Side cutters

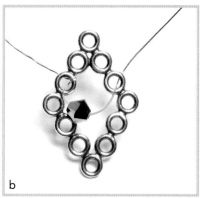

a

b

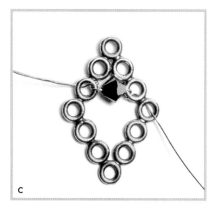

c

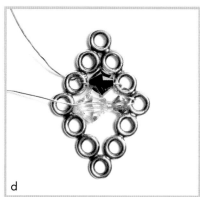

d

necklace

1 Attach the wire to the interior of the hole by wrapping two to three times **(a)**. (For this project, it's best to cut the wire individually for each component, depending on the size of the component and how densely you plan to position the beaded rows. For example, the smallest component with a single bead will only require an inch of wire, while the largest component with multiple rows of beads can use up to 6 in./15cm of wire.)

2 String a bead or beads onto the wire **(b)**. String the wire through the hole on the opposite side of the component and wrap the wire around the side of the hole once **(c)**.

3 String the wire through the next hole and wrap around the side of the hole once. Then string a bead or beads onto the wire **(d)**.

4 Continue this pattern for as many rows as needed, adapting to the shape of each filigree component.

5 Finish the component by wrapping the wire around the side of the hole. Trim the excess wire and tuck it in with chainnose pliers **(e)**.

6 Make 16 components of varying sizes and shapes.

7 Cut the chain into 16 2-in. (5cm) pieces.

8 Use jump rings to connect all of the components, alternating them with chain **(f)**.

58

e

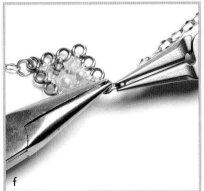

f

g

h

i

✳ More About the Fresh Look

The same delicate filigree takes on a substantial look when paired with the bracelet's oversized textured links.

earrings

9 Make a beaded component as in steps 1–5 of the necklace (g).

10 Cut a two-link piece of chain.

11 String a crystal on a headpin and attach it to the piece of chain with a wrapped loop (h).

12 Use a jump ring to attach the chain/crystal component to the bottom hole of the filigree component (i).

13 Connect the earring wire to the top of the component with two jump rings.

14 Make a second earring (if you prefer symmetrical earrings, you can mirror the design of the first earring).

Sparkling Pearl
necklace & earrings

CLASSIC Style

A single color can make a striking statement. Here, the white tones and bright metal of the sparkling pearl set give a formal and elegant look.

Fresh LOOK

Changing the color palette from monochrome to variegated, and choosing a bolder, darker chain, updates this look. Though both of the necklaces have cascading drops, the earthy gemstone set uses an asymmetrical pattern with different lengths for a more modern effect. The multicolored round stones give the necklace depth and tie in the various gemstone drops.

materials

necklace

- **11** crystal-inlaid pearls
- **13** 5mm pearls
- **13** 1½-in. (3.8cm) 24-gauge headpins
- **2** jump rings
- **2** crimp tubes
- **2** crimp covers
- 2 in. (5cm) large-link extender chain
- 40 in. (102cm) fine-link chain
- 5 in. (13cm) flexible beading wire
- Hook clasp

earrings

- **2** crystal-inlaid pearls
- **2** 1½-in. (3.8cm) 24-gauge headpins
- **2** jump rings
- 3 in. (7.6cm) fine-link chain
- Pair of textured earring wires

tools

- Roundnose pliers
- Chainnose pliers
- Flatnose pliers
- Crimping pliers
- Side cutters
- Flexible beading wire cutters

a

b

c

d

e

necklace

1 Cut six 1¼-in. (3.2cm), five 1⅝-in. (4.1cm), and two 7–8-in. (18–20cm) pieces of chain **(a)**.

2 String all of the inlaid pearls on headpins (one pearl per headpin) and attach each to a 1¼-in. or 1⅝-in. piece of chain with a wrapped loop **(b)**.

3 On flexible beading wire, string: a 5mm pearl, a shorter piece of chain with pearl, a 5mm pearl, and a long piece of chain with pearl. Repeat the pattern until you have used all the chain/pearl components. End with a 5mm pearl **(c)**.

4 String a crimp and one of the long pieces of chain on one end of the flexible beading wire. Go back through the crimp tube and crimp **(d)**. Repeat on the other end with the other long piece of chain.

5 Slide the crimp cover over the crimp and use chainnose pliers to gently squeeze it together until closed **(e)**. Repeat for the other crimp.

6 Attach the hook to one side of the necklace with a jump ring. Attach the extender chain to the other side of the necklace with a jump ring. String a 5mm pearl on a headpin and attach it to the end of the extender chain with a wrapped loop.

earrings

7 Cut two 1¼-in. pieces of chain.

8 String a pearl on a headpin and attach it to the end of one of the pieces of chain with a wrapped loop. Attach the other end of the chain piece to the earring wire with a jump ring.

9 Make a second earring.

More About the Fresh Look

The beauty in this design is that anything goes. It's a great way to use up stray beads.

Victorian Classic
necklace

CLASSIC Style

The draped double chain, the filigree settings, the pearl in the focal piece, and the symmetrically placed fresh water pearl drops are all iconic elements of Victorian jewelry.

Fresh LOOK

Curving a large filigree component into a bracelet gives an edgier, more ornate feel. The sparkling rivoli crystal is set in the same way as the mabé pearl in the classic design. I strung wire through the adjacent openings of two opposite corners, centered the component on the filigree and wrapped them together. I finished the bracelet with jump

materials

NOTE: All metal components are antiqued brass.

- 16–18mm mabé pearl
- 10–12mm teardrop pearl
- **15** 4–5mm pearls
- 1⅜-in. (3.5cm) six-petal filigree component
- Filigree bead cap
- **16** headpins
- **8** 5mm jump rings
- 3 ft. (.90cm) chain
- Lobster claw clasp

tools

- Chainnose pliers
- Roundnose pliers
- Flatnose pliers
- Side cutters

a

b

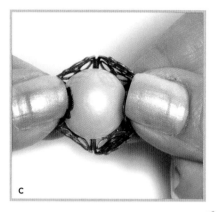

c

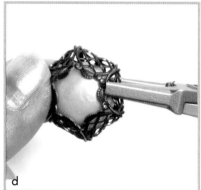

d

e

1 Cut the chain into two 8-in. (20cm) pieces, two 8¼-in. (21cm) pieces, and one 2-in. (5cm) piece.

2 Use flatnose pliers to flatten the filigree component **(a)**. Use the pliers again to bend the petals slightly upward.

3 Using flatnose pliers, make a 90-degree bend in each petal, as shown, to make a setting **(b)**.

4 Insert the mabé pearl into the setting and hold firmly while you bend the petals over the pearl with your fingers. Work in pairs, bending facing petals at the same time **(c)**.

5 Use flatnose pliers to tighten the petals against the pearl **(d)**.

6 String an open jump ring through two adjacent openings on a point of the setting and close it **(e)**.

f

g

h

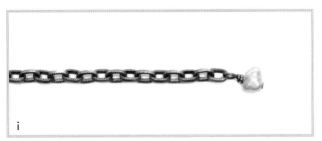

i

j

7 String a pearl and a bead cap onto a headpin and make a wrapped loop. Attach the pearl component to the jump ring from step 6 with a jump ring **(f)**.

8 String an open jump ring through two adjacent openings at the point shown. String an 8- and an 8¼-in. piece of chain on the jump ring (so the 8-in. piece is the inner strand) and close the jump ring **(g)**. Repeat on the other side of the pendant.

9 Slide a jump ring through both end links of the chain on one end and close it. Repeat on the other end. Use a jump ring to attach a clasp on one end **(h)**. On the other end, use a jump ring to attach the 2-in. piece of chain. String a pearl onto a headpin and attach it to the end of the chain with a wrapped loop **(i)**.

10 String a pearl onto a headpin and connect it to the outside chain with a wrapped loop. Repeat to attach seven dangles on each side of the pendant **(j)**.

More About the Fresh Look
Filigree components are generally flat. Look at them with a little imagination, however, and you'll see they can be curved, used to bezel stones, formed into bracelets as I've done here, and even made into rings.

Promise Ring lariat

CLASSIC Style

My twist on the classic bridal lariat? A promise ring is the main design element. It gives the necklace a special sentimental significance and a romantic Victorian feel.

Fresh LOOK

The ocean inspired the variation: Various tones of green and dark iridescent pearls reflect the colors of the water and the black sand beaches of Hawaii. The ends are finished with Roman glass, tumbled smooth by the ages just as beach glass is smoothed by waves and sand. The ring is recycled from a bottle, and its green translucence recalls the waters of the sea.

materials

materials

- 20mm ring with loop
- **50–60** 3–8mm Swarovski crystals
- **50–60** 3–6mm pearls
- **20–30** 5x2mm fine silver beads
- 13º charlottes
- **2** 4mm daisy spacers
- **2** 9x11mm floral bead caps
- **2** 2-in. (5cm) 24-gauge headpins
- **2** crimp tubes
- **2** crimp covers
- 80 in. (2m) flexible beading wire

tools

- Roundnose pliers
- Chainnose pliers
- Crimping pliers
- Side cutters
- Flexible beading wire cutters

More About the Fresh Look

There are many ways to wear a lariat: Long, with both ends through the ring, doubled into a shorter necklace with both ends trailing in the same direction, or even as a belt. Have fun experimenting with a fresh look of your own.

a

b

c

d

e

f

1 On a headpin, string: a 3mm bicone crystal, a daisy spacer, a 6mm glass pearl, a bead cap, and a 3mm bicone crystal. Make a wrapped loop above the beads **(a)**. Repeat to make a second headpin component.

2 String and center 10–14 charlottes on flexible beading wire **(b)**.

3 String the loop on the ring and center it over the charlottes. String a 6mm glass pearl over both wire ends. Snug the pearl to the charlottes **(c)**.

4 Separate the strands, and string each with a variety of beads. Create short pattern groups within the longer design. Break up some of the groupings with larger beads. Try to keep the strands interesting by varying the patterns that are adjacent to each other **(d)**. String one end approximately 1–1½ in. (2.5–3.8cm) longer than the other.

5 Crimp each end of the lariat to a headpin component **(e)**.

6 Slide the crimp cover over the crimp and use chainnose pliers to gently squeeze it together until closed **(f)**. Repeat for the other crimp.

Cascading Crystals
necklace

CLASSIC Style

The crystal necklace features traditional elements of jewelry design such as bright metals, a heart pendant, and Swarovski crystals.

Fresh **LOOK**

The variation plays with a found-object motif. I used several different kinds of beads: some faceted, some polished, and some matte. An eclectic mix of components, including a coin, filigree pieces, and a vine link, build on the theme. The varied and asymmetrical lengths of chain, the color palette, and the non-traditional metal create an earthy, casual design.

materials

NOTE: All crystal and rhinestone components are Swarovski Elements.

- 14x18mm crystal heart drop
- 10x18mm large De Art crystal drop
- 9x14mm small De Art crystal drop
- 6x9mm crystal teardrop
- 6mm crystal cube
- 6mm round crystal
- a few 5mm bicone crystals
- a few 4mm bicone crystals
- **5–8** 3mm bicone crystals
- 5mm crystal rondelle
- 6mm rhinestone squaredelle
- 4mm rhinestone rondelle
- **4–6** 2mm silver beads
- **5** 9mm twisted wire rings
- **9** 6mm jump rings
- **3** 24-gauge headpins
- **2** pinch ends with prongs (3mm interior diameter)
- 4¾ in. (12cm) fine-link chain
- 2 in. (5cm) large-link extender chain
- 18–20 in. (46–51cm) SilverSilk capture chain
- 6 in. (15cm) 28-gauge craft wire
- 4 in. (10cm) 24-gauge silver-filled wire
- Hook clasp

tools

- Roundnose pliers
- Chainnose pliers
- Flatnose pliers
- Side cutters

a

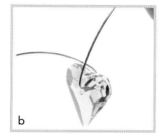

b

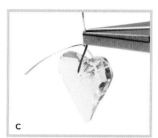

c

d

e

f

g

h

i

1 Cut the fine-link chain into 15¾-, 12-, 8-, 6-, and 3⅛-in. (40, 30, 20, 15, and 8cm) pieces.

2 String the heart drop about 1 in. (2.5cm) from the end of the 24-gauge wire **(a)**.

3 Bend both sides of the wire upward and slightly curve them so they form a triangle **(b)**.

4 At the intersection of the two wires, bend the long end of the wire up so that it lines up with the heart drop. Bend the short end of the wire so that it is perpendicular to the long end **(c)**.

5 Wrap the short end around the long end three times. Trim the excess wire **(d)** and tuck it in using chainnose pliers **(e)**.

6 String a 4mm rondelle onto the wire and connect it to the 40mm piece of chain with a wrapped loop **(f, g)**.

7 On a headpin, string a 5mm bicone, a rhinestone squardelle, and a crystal cube bead. Connect it to the 30mm piece of chain with a wrapped loop **(h)**.

8 On a headpin, string a 4mm bicone, a rhinestone rondelle, and a teardrop bead and connect it to the 20mm piece of chain with a wrapped loop **(i)**.

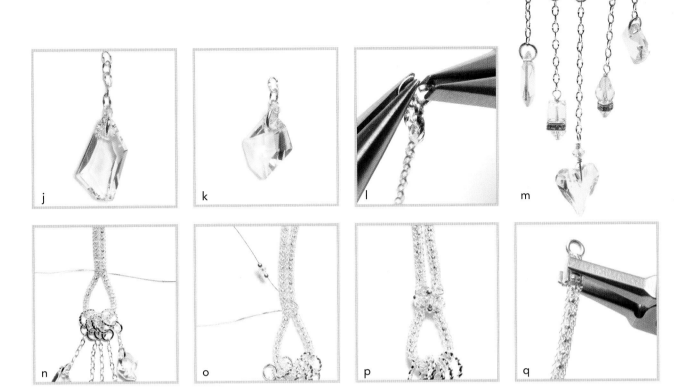

9 Use a jump ring to attach the large baroque drop to the 15mm chain piece **(j)**.

10 Use a jump ring to attach the small baroque drop to the 8mm chain piece **(k)**.

11 Use jump rings to attach each of the crystal/chain components to the twisted wire rings **(l)**.

12 String the capture chain through the twisted wire rings, arranging the crystal/chain components as shown **(m)**.

13 Center the focal point components on the capture chain.

14 Wrap the 28-gauge wire once around both sides of the capture chain 20–25mm from the center on either side. Bring the wire ends to the front and begin to add 3mm bicones and 2mm silver beads. This is a freeform wrap. Use as many beads and go around as many times as it takes to create a secure and attractive wrap **(n–p)**.

15 Insert an end of the capture chain into the pinch end as far as it will go (you may need to open the pinch end slightly wider than it already is using flatnose pliers). Use flatnose pliers to firmly close the pinch end, first closing one pair of "petals," and then the other **(q)**.

16 Use a jump ring to connect a hook clasp to one of the pinch ends and an extender chain to the other. String a 6mm crystal onto a headpin and attach it to the extender chain with a wrapped loop.

More About the Fresh Look

A coin is a fun and versatile component. I used hole-punching pliers to punch the connector holes and create the dangle.

Gemstone
ring

CLASSIC Style

Nothing is more classic than a prong-set gemstone, especially a single prong-set gemstone ring. This look has been popular for many years, and I've created my own classic version using wire.

Fresh LOOK

For the variation, I used the same technique to create the ring, except instead of using a prong setting, I left the center open. I domed and textured a metal blank, and then punched holes so I could attach it to the ring shank with heavy-gauge headpins. This clean, contemporary design with contrasting materials creates a look with an urban, edgy feel.

* materials

- 6mm gemstone (lab-created spinel)
- 6mm prong setting
- 10 in. (25cm) 18-gauge half-hard wire

tools

- Roundnose pliers
- Flatnose pliers
- Side cutters
- Ring mandrel
- Pencil

a

b

c

d

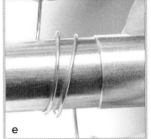

e

f

g

h

i

1 Place the gemstone flat side down **(a)**. Put the prong setting over the gemstone and use the eraser side of a pencil to snap it in place **(b)**.

2 String the wire through the center opening of the gemstone setting so that the gemstone setting is centered on the wire **(c)**.

3 Place the wire with the gemstone over the desired size on the ring mandrel. Bend each end of the wire all the way around the ring mandrel, bringing them alongside the gemstone **(d, e)**.

4 Wrap each of the wire ends around the gemstone **(f)**.

5 Wrap each wire end once around the ring shank **(g)**.

6 Use roundnose pliers to begin a spiral at one end of the wire **(h)**. Use flatnose pliers to complete the spiral **(i)**. Repeat on the other wire end.

* More About the Fresh Look

The type of headpin you select for this project sets the tone for the ring. For a little extra sparkle, use Swarovski crystal headpins in this design.

Textured
earrings

CLASSIC Style

Traditionally, mixed-metals jewelry combines silver and gold, and the two colors complement each other. These textured earrings create a harmonious blend of the two, with a traditional teardrop shape as a silhouetted backdrop.

Fresh LOOK

The variation uses a more modern combination of copper and silver, and the very rich patina on the copper creates a greater contrast between the metals. I've mixed shapes and also varied the sizes of the spirals. Jump rings hinge the pieces together to give movement. Even though the texturing is similar, different metals and patinas create a bolder look.

materials

- **2** 16x22mm sterling silver teardrop blanks
- **8** 5mm jump rings
- **2** 3-in. (7.6cm) lengths of 18-gauge gold-filled wire
- **2** gold-filled earring wires

tools and supplies

- Roundnose pliers
- Chainnose pliers
- 1.8mm hole-punch pliers
- Side cutters
- Bench block
- Chasing hammer
- Polishing pad
- Tweezers
- Liver of sulfur
- Small bowl

a

b

c

d

e

f

1 Place a silver blank on a bench block. Use the ball side of the chasing hammer to texture the entire blank **(a)**.

2 Use a liver of sulfur solution to add patina to the silver blank **(b)**.

3 Use an abrasive pad to polish the silver blank **(c)**.

4 Use hole-punch pliers to punch a hole approximately 2mm from the top of the silver blank **(d, e)**.

5 Repeat steps 1–4 with the remaining silver blank.

6 Use chainnose pliers to make a spiral at the end of a gold-filled wire, making certain that it fits within and is proportional to the shape and size of the blank **(f)**.

g

h

i

j

k

❋
More About the Fresh Look

When using liver of sulfur to add patina to copper, be sure to keep the sediment or any undissolved liver of sulfur pieces from touching the metal, or it will cause an undesirable blackening that is difficult to remove. Copper oxidizes much faster than silver does. Dip the copper piece quickly several times until the desired color is achieved.

7 Hammer the spiral with a chasing hammer while holding the end of the wire (do not hammer the end of the wire) **(g)**.

8 Bend the wire at the top of the spiral and make a loop **(h, i)**.

9 Repeat steps 6–8 to make a second spiral the mirror image of the first.

10 Use two jump rings to connect a spiral component to a silver component through the hole **(j)**. Repeat with the remaining components.

11 Connect the earring wire with two jump rings **(k)**. Repeat to finish the second earring.

Heirloom
Filigree
pendant

CLASSIC Style

Placing the filigree component on the diagonal makes a traditional diamond shape. The cascade of drops at the bottom completes the classic look.

Fresh LOOK

I wanted the variation to have a bolder, edgier feel, so I used a slightly larger rivoli and I changed the positioning of the filigree component to a square. I added different antiqued metal components and textures, and I used two strands of metallic leather cord to give the necklace bolder lines.

materials

- 12mm Swarovski rivoli
- **3** 5x9mm Swarovski briolettes
- 20mm large square filigree component
- 15x18mm small filigree component
- 10mm textured ring
- **11** 5mm jump rings
- Cable chain cut into 6, 12, and 18mm pieces
- 28 gauge wire

tools

- Chainnose pliers
- Flatnose pliers
- Bail-making pliers
- Side cutters

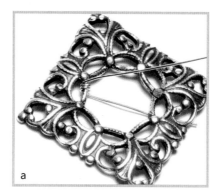
a

b

c

d

e

f

g

More About the Fresh Look

I used two-hole spacer bars to guide the leather cord and create a loop to connect to the centerpiece. Then I finished the ends by wrapping them in wire and inserting them into a pinch-end component.

1 Secure the wire by wrapping it two to three times around the sections of the inner frame of the large filigree component, with the long end of the wire exiting toward the front **(a, b)**.

2 Place the rivoli on top of the filigree component **(c)**.

3 Moving clockwise, string the wire over the top of the rivoli, skipping two of the inner frame sections, and going down into the third section of the filigree component **(d)**. String the wire counterclockwise through the adjacent opening, back to front **(e)**. Continue this pattern until you have gone all the way around the rivoli and have completed a square pattern **(f, g)**.

4 String the wires counterclockwise from back to front of the filigree component, and continue as in step 3 to create a second square pattern on top of the first **(h–k)**. Secure the ends of the wire at the back of the filigree component. Trim and tuck in the excess wire on both ends.

h

i

j

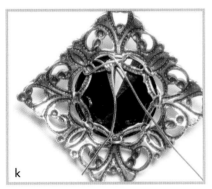

k

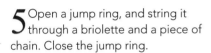

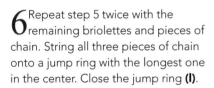

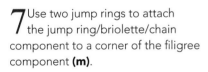

l

m

5 Open a jump ring, and string it through a briolette and a piece of chain. Close the jump ring.

6 Repeat step 5 twice with the remaining briolettes and pieces of chain. String all three pieces of chain onto a jump ring with the longest one in the center. Close the jump ring **(l)**.

7 Use two jump rings to attach the jump ring/briolette/chain component to a corner of the filigree component **(m)**.

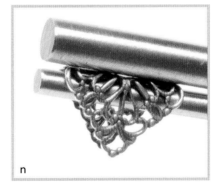

n

o

8 To make the bail, use bail-making pliers to bend the small filigree component **(n)**. Use two jump rings to attach the bail to a large decorative ring **(o)**.

9 Use three jump rings to attach the large decorative ring to the large filigree component **(p)**.

p

Sparkle
Cubed
pendant & earrings

CLASSIC Style

A traditional geometric style and a symmetrical cube motif marks this classic component that is repeated throughout the pendant and earrings.

Fresh
LOOK

The variation has more lively movement. I used a large patterned ring instead of a traditional bail and added more geometric shapes for an asymmetrical design with vibrant colors.

materials

pendant
- **4** 16-hole filigree components
- 8mm crystal cube
- 4mm round crystals:
    - **12** color A
    - **12** color B
    - **12** color C
- **2** 4mm crystal bicones
- Headpin
- **4** 5mm jump rings
- Bail
- 3 in. (7.6cm) 22-gauge wire
- 12 in. (30cm) 28-gauge craft wire

earrings
- **6** 9-hole filigree components
- 4mm round crystals:
    - **9** color B
    - **9** color C
- **6** 4mm crystal bicones
- **4** headpins
- **4** 5mm jump rings
- **2** ½-in. (3cm) pieces of chain
- **2** 8-in. lengths of 28-gauge craft wire
- Pair of earring wires

tools
- Chainnose pliers
- Flatnose pliers
- Side cutters

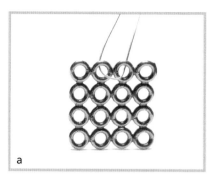
a

b

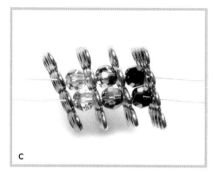

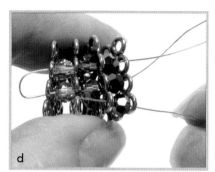

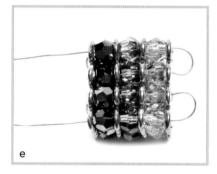
c

d

e

f

pendant

1 Bend the 12-in. (30cm) wire length in half. String both ends of the wire through adjacent holes of a square filigree component **(a)**.

2 String a color A round crystal onto each wire end. String a square filigree component onto each wire end so the second filigree component lines up with the first. String a color B round crystal onto each wire end. String a filigree component. Align this component with the first two **(b)**.

3 String a color C round crystal onto each wire end. String a filigree component. Align this component with the first three **(c)**.

4 String each wire end through adjacent holes in the filigree components **(d)**, and continue stringing crystals, reversing the order of the crystal colors so they line up within each row. Repeat until you strung crystals around the entire cube **(e)**.

5 String each end of the wire through at least one more row of crystals. Trim the ends, leaving a ⅜-in. (10mm) wire tail exiting the bead **(f)**.

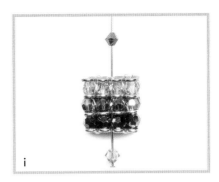

g

h

i

j

k

l

m

6 Bend the wire toward the next crystal and use chainnose pliers to bend it over the crystal hole **(g)**. Push the end of the wire into the crystal **(h)**.

7 String a bicone crystal onto a headpin. String the headpin through the center of the cube. String a bicone crystal **(i)** and make a wrapped loop **(j)**.

8 Make a wrapped loop on each end of the 8mm crystal cube **(k)**. Attach the beaded cube component to the 8mm crystal cube component with two jump rings. Attach the 8mm crystal cube component to the bail with two jump rings **(l)**.

earrings

9 Make a beaded component using the smaller filigree components and only two layers of crystal (I used colors B and C). Make two **(m)**.

10 String a bicone crystal on a headpin. String the headpin through the center of the beaded cube. String another bicone crystal and make a wrapped loop.

11 Attach the beaded bead component to one end of the piece of chain with two jump rings. Make a bicone crystal/headpin component.

12 String the end chain link and the bicone crystal/headpin component onto an earring wire.

13 Make a second earring.

More About the Fresh Look
Make sure the filigree components you select for this technique have an obvious center for the headpin or wire to go through (not all of them do).

Orbital
Spinner
ring

CLASSIC Style

Spinner rings have been popular for years. To create my version of the design, I used a single round bead as the main element for an elegant and traditional look, and I paired it with a commercially available shank for a polished design.

Fresh LOOK

The variation has an organic, handmade look. I made the shank out of heavy-gauge, hammered wire. I accented the wire ends with spirals that also created a hole for the headpin to pass through. This copper art bead by Patricia Healey has a beautiful torch patina that gives the metal a terrific depth and luster. Paired with the silver of the shank, it creates a modern and bold contrast. A set of dangles on one side gives a touch of asymmetry, sparkle, and motion.

materials

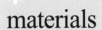

- 12mm rhinestone ball
- **2** ball-end headpins
- Ring shank

tools

- Chainnose pliers
- Flatnose pliers
- Side cutters
- Ring mandrel

a

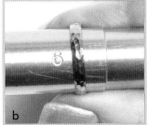

b

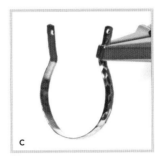

c

d

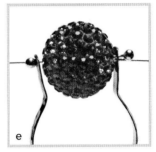

e

f

1 Wrap the ring shank around the ring mandrel, starting one to two sizes smaller than the desired ring size **(a, b)**. Because the ring blank is made out of work-hardened metal, it will spring outward after being wrapped around the mandrel. You may need to use chainnose pliers to adjust the ring to the correct size.

2 Using flatnose pliers, bend both ends of the ring blank upwards approximately 5/16 in. (8mm) from the end so they are parallel to each other **(c)**.

3 String a ball-end headpin through one of the holes in the ring blank, then through a rhinestone bead, then through the other hole in the ring blank **(d)**.

4 Repeat step 3, working from the opposite direction **(e)**.

5 Adjust the headpins to leave a space of approximately 2mm between the ball end and the ring shank on each side.

6 Bend each end of the ball-end headpin opposite the ball end, flush against the ring shank **(f)**.

7 Wrap each end of the ball-end headpins around the opposite ball-end headpin two to three times to fill the gap.

8 Trim the excess wire and tuck it in using chainnose pliers.

More About the Fresh Look

The beauty of making your own shank is that you are in complete control of sizing and are able to adjust it to accommodate a large bead like this one.

87

Buttoned
Up bracelet

CLASSIC Style

This design contains
a hint of inspiration
from a tennis bracelet in
its geometric and

Fresh LOOK

Adding a variety of filigree components in different
styles and shapes to the framed button elements
creates a much more Bohemian feel, rich with
texture and color, reminiscent of stringing together
various treasures collected from an antique store.

materials

- **6** 12mm square crystal buttons
- **6** metal frame components with granulation detail
- **64** 5mm jump rings
- **14** 4x8mm figure-8 chain links
- **6** 8-in. (20cm) lengths of 28-gauge craft wire
- Toggle clasp

tools

- Chainnose pliers
- Flatnose pliers
- Side cutters

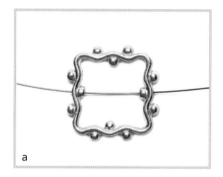

a

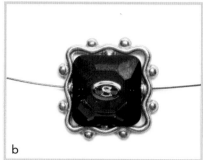

b

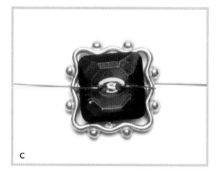

c

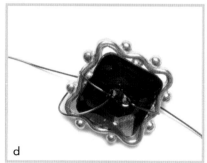

d

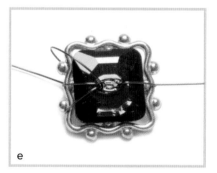

e

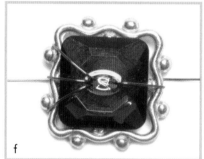

f

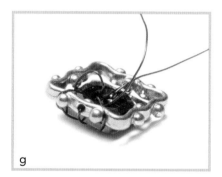

g

1 Center a frame component on a wire **(a)**.

2 Place the crystal button on top of the frame component so the buttonholes line up with the wire **(b)**.

3 String a wire end through a crystal hole from front to back. Repeat with the other wire end **(c)**.

4 Bring a wire end around a granulation detail on the frame and back through the same hole, front to back **(d)**. Repeat with the other end.

5 Bring a wire end around another granulation detail and back through the same hole again **(e)**. Repeat with the other end. Each crystal hole will have three wraps, evenly spaced around the detail on the frame edge **(f)**.

6 Working with the same end of the wire, bundle the two wire lengths that go around the granulation details **(g)**. Use the tip of chainnose pliers to hold the end of the wire and wrap it around three to four times. Trim the excess wire and tuck it in toward the crystal button. Repeat with the other end. (Front view of the completed crystal button component **(h)** and back view **(i)**.)

h

i

j

k

l

m

7 Repeat steps 1–6 to create five more crystal button and frame components.

8 Attach two jump rings to each corner of each crystal button component **(j)**.

9 Unlink the figure-8 links (like opening a jump ring) **(k)**. Use the figure-8 chain links to connect all of the components through the jump rings **(l)**.

10 Add another set of figure-8 chain links and another set of two jump rings to each of the remaining corners.

11 On each end, connect all four jump rings with an additional two jump rings.

12 Use a set of two jump rings to attach a toggle clasp ring to one end of the bracelet and a bar to the other **(m)**.

More About the Fresh Look

To create just the right curve for a necklace, you might have to experiment with the length of chain pieces and jump rings you use in the outer edge. The outside length will always be longer than the inside length.

Framed Gems
set

CLASSIC Style

I love the possibilities of the stacked components in these designs. Clear CZs as the central elements really shine: The jewelry has a bright, sparkling clarity and looks polished and formal.

Fresh LOOK

For the variation, framing a single component and making it a centerpiece creates more drama . A CZ in a darker color framed with a gunmetal ring gives contrast in the shape as well as the color of the metal. A ribbon with variegated charcoal tones reflects the color of the ring and gives it a casual yet elegant finish.

materials

earrings
- **2** 12x8mm CZ drops
- **2** 11mm square CZs
- **2** square filigree components
- **4** 4mm aluminum jump rings
- 28-gauge craft wire
- pair of earring wires

pendant
- 12x8mm CZ drop
- 11mm square CZ
- **2** square filigree components
- **8** 3mm Swarovski round crystals
- **6** 4mm aluminum jump rings
- Bail
- 28-gauge craft wire

bracelet
- **7** 11mm square CZs
- **14** square filigree components
- **56** 3mm Swarovski round crystals
- **32** 4mm aluminum jump rings
- 28-gauge craft wire
- Toggle clasp

tools and supplies
- Chainnose pliers
- Flatnose pliers
- Side cutters

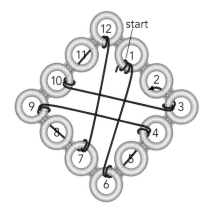

fig. 1

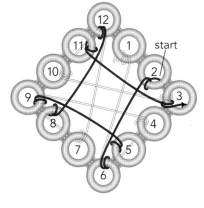

fig. 2

earrings

1 Cut an 8-in. (20 cm) length of craft wire. Wrap the end around the interior side of hole 1 of the filigree component.

2 Hold the stone firmly on top of the filigree component. You will be wrapping the wire across the component to secure it in the following pattern **(fig. 1)**. As you come through each new hole, wrap the wire to secure it.

- String from hole 1 across the component and through hole 6 from front to back.

- String from hole 6 through hole 4 from back to front.

- String from hole 4 through hole 9 from front to back.

- String from hole 9 to hole 7 from back to front.

- String from hole 7 to hole 12 from front to back.

- String from hole 12 to hole 10 from back to front.

- String from hole 10 to hole 3 from front to back.

At this point, you've gone around the entire component and the wire is going through hole 3 from front to back.

3 String from hole 3 through hole 2, back to front. As in step two, you will be wrapping the wire across the component to secure it in the following pattern **(fig. 2)**. As you come through each new hole, wrap the wire to secure it.

- String from hole 2 to hole 6 from front to back.

- String from hole 6 to hole 5 from back to front.

- String from hole 5 to hole 9 from front to back.

- String from hole 9 to hole 8 from back to front.

- String from hole 8 to hole 12 from front to back.

- String from hole 12 to hole 11 from back to front.

- String from hole 11 to hole 3 from front to back. Wrap the wire around 3.

4 Trim the wire and tuck it in toward the stone using chainnose pliers **(a)**.

5 Connect a jump ring to a CZ drop **(b)**.

6 Connect two jump rings to the bottom corner of a component **(c)**.

7 Use a jump ring to connect the CZ/component to the two jump rings **(d)**.

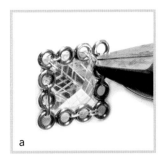

a

b

c

d

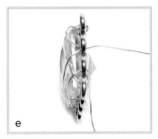

e

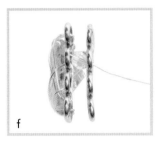

f

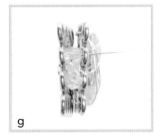

g

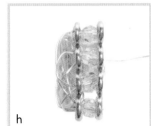

h

i

j

8 Attach the dangle to an earring wire. Make a second earring.

pendant

9 Make two squares following steps 1–3 of the earrings, but use 12 in. (30cm) of wire.

10 After completing two squares, the wire will be at the back of the stone. Bring the wire from the back to the front between the holes. String the wire from front to back through the second hole from the corner **(e)**.

11 String a 3mm crystal and another filigree component through the same loop (the second hole from the corner) **(f)**.

12 String from back to front through the next opening in the component, adding another crystal. Then string through the original component **(g)**.

13 Go around the corner of the stone, skipping the corner hole of the component and repeat steps 13 and 14.

14 Continue this pattern until all sides of the stacked component are finished.

15 String the wire through an adjacent bead to bring it to the back **(h)**.

16 Cut and tuck in the wire using chainnose pliers **(i)**.

17 Repeat step 7 to attach the CZ drop through the front square of the filigree component.

18 Attach the bail to the front square of the stacked component using two jump rings.

k

l

bracelet

19 Repeat steps 9-14 seven times to make seven stacked components.

20 Attach a pair of jump rings to opposite corner holes of each component (front component only) **(j)**.

21 Connect all components with another pair of jump rings **(k)**.

22 Attach the toggle rings and bar on each end with a pair of jump rings **(l)**.

More About the Fresh Look

Centering the focal piece inside the ring can be challenging. Try using two or four pieces of wire and alternating sides to keep the tension even as you continue wrapping.

Stacked Solitaire
ring

CLASSIC Style

A solitaire diamond ring is steeped in tradition. Popular for over a century, it usually features a single stone. Mine is a variation, with a large Swarovski crystal as the central element and smaller crystals structured underneath to echo the round shape of the crystal.

Fresh LOOK

Combining different metals and bringing the wire to the forefront of the design gives the ring an industrial look. A touch of steampunk comes from the gear components, and the red crystal in the center provides a Gothic element. The ring is slightly over-sized, which is more contemporary, and the layering creates visual interest.

materials

- 14mm Swarovski crystal button
- **10** 4mm crystal round beads
- **2** 10-hole round filigree components
- Ring shank
- 28-gauge craft wire cut into one
  14-in. (36cm) and two 5-in. (13cm)
  lengths

tools

- Chainnose pliers
- Side cutters

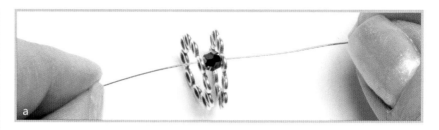

a

b

c

d

1 String the 14-in. (36cm) length of wire through one of the holes of a filigree component. String a crystal and one hole of the second filigree component **(a)**.

2 String the wire back through an adjacent hole of the filigree component, string a crystal, and go through a corresponding hole of the other filigree component **(b)**.

3 Continue until you have strung wire through and beaded between all of the holes **(c)**.

4 String through the adjacent beads with both wire ends, continuing in opposite directions, until the two ends of the wire are opposite one another with four holes between them on each side **(d)**.

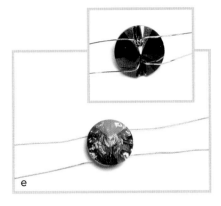

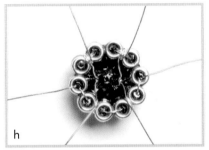

e

f

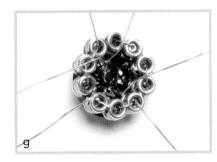

g

h

i

j

k

5 String two 5-in. (13cm) wire lengths through the button shank **(e)**. Pull all four ends of the wire through the stacked crystal and filigree component **(f)**.

6 Separate the two wire lengths so each pair of wire ends faces in opposite directions **(g)**.

7 Wrap each end tightly around the bottom of the stacked filigree component as shown **(h)**.

8 Trim **(i)** and tuck in the excess wire **(j)** on all four wire ends.

9 Use the wire ends coming out of the crystals of the stacked filigree component to firmly wrap the stacked filigree component onto the ring shank **(k)**. You may need to weave the wire in and out of the stacked filigree component several times. Trim and tuck in the excess wire.

Floral Wrist
corsage

CLASSIC Style

The bright metal bracelet has a lush floral outline at its center. Accented with clear and light-colored crystals, it sparkles with a polished, classic look that is romantic and elegant.

Fresh LOOK

The variation boasts an edgier, Gothic-flavored design featuring black and metallic crystals and nontraditional metal accents. The resulting bracelet has a hint of steampunk and a more striking central element.

materials

- 24mm Lucite flower
- **5** 8–12mm Lucite flowers
- **2** 10mm Swarovski round crystals
- **50–60** 2–6mm assorted shape Swarovski crystals
- **12** 4mm daisy spacers
- **2** 7mm jump rings
- 52 in. (132cm) 24-gauge silver craft wire
- 12–14 in. (30–36cm) SilverSilk netted tubing
- **2** double pinch ends
- Toggle clasp

tools and supplies

- Chainnose pliers
- Flatnose pliers
- Side cutters
- G-S Hypo Cement

More About the Fresh Look

Bell-shaped pinch ends lend themselves beautifully to finishing netted tubing. They are just the right size for the ends and no glue is required.

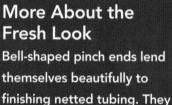

a

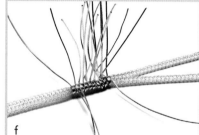

b

c

d

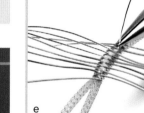

e

f

g

1 Cut the wire into eight 4-in. (10cm) and two 10-in. (25cm) lengths. Cut the netted tubing into two 6–7-in. (15–18cm) pieces.

2 Place the two pieces of netted tubing side by side. Center a 4-in. wire length under the tubing and wrap it around twice **(a)**. It is easiest to begin wrapping with your hands, then tighten with chainnose pliers **(b)**. Repeat with all the 4-in. lengths **(c)**. When you are finished, all the wire ends should be on the same side (the top) and the portion that is wire wrapped should be centered on the netted tubing.

3 Wrap the 10-in. wire lengths on either side of the wirewrapped portion of the netted tubing, leaving one end longer than the other (approximately 6-in. long) **(d)**.

4 Using chainnose pliers, bend all wire ends up, with the exception of the two long ends **(e, f)**.

102

h

i

j

k

l

m

5 Gather three of the central wires and string them through the 24mm Lucite flower **(g)**. Gently pull the wires to tighten the flower.

6 String a crystal on each of the wires in the center of the flower **(h)**. Bend the wire over using chainnose pliers **(i)**. Trim the excess wire and pinch the wire into place with chainnose pliers **(j)**. This will create a faux loop.

7 Continue to string crystals and Lucite flowers, using them singly or stacking them, and finish them with faux loops **(k)**.

8 After the 4-in. wire ends are beaded, bead the shorter ends of the 10-in. wire lengths and use the end of the wire to go around one piece of netted tubing **(l)**. Anchor the wire by wrapping it around itself. Trim the excess wire and tuck in with chainnose pliers **(m)**.

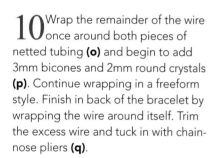

9 Split the two pieces of netted tubing on one side. Position the remaining wire between them. String an assortment of 10mm round crystals, 6mm rondelles, 4mm bicones, and daisy spacers until you reach approximately 1½ in. (40cm) **(n)**.

10 Wrap the remainder of the wire once around both pieces of netted tubing **(o)** and begin to add 3mm bicones and 2mm round crystals **(p)**. Continue wrapping in a freeform style. Finish in back of the bracelet by wrapping the wire around itself. Trim the excess wire and tuck in with chain-nose pliers **(q)**.

11 Repeat steps 9 and 10 on the other end.

12 Put a small amount of G-S Hypo Cement at the end of each piece of netted tubing **(r)**. Insert the tubing ends into the double pinch end as far as it will go and use flatnose pliers to firmly close the pinch end **(s)**. Repeat for the other end.

13 Use jump rings to attach the clasp to each end of the bracelet **(t)**.

Bora Bora Pearl
earrings

CLASSIC Style

The beautiful luster and round shape of Tahitian pearls add a sophisticated touch to any design. As in the South Seas Necklace project, I've used shell pearls to echo the look of Tahitian pearls, and the earrings have elegant curves and classic lines.

Fresh LOOK

The variation is very similar in construction, but changing the materials gives the piece an entirely new feel. The necklace features mixed metals and antiqued brass tones, and instead of a pearl, there is a Victorian-inspired filigree leaf element. The curved component resembles a vine, and the whole piece has a touch of industrial chic. The colors of the metals give it a casual look.

a

b

c

d

e

f

g

h

i

materials

- **2** 10mm shell pearls
- **2** headpins
- **6** jump rings
- **4** 3-in. (7.6cm) pieces of 18-gauge wire
- Pair of earring wires

tools

- Roundnose pliers
- Chainnose pliers
- Large stepped wire-wrapping pliers
- Side cutters
- Chasing hammer
- Bench block

More About the Fresh Look

Wrapping wire in a contrasting color over another adds texture and depth to your design.

1 Use the middle step of the large stepped wire-wrapping pliers to create a curve at the end of one piece of wire (this will be the top of the component) **(a)**.

2 Use the large step of the wire-wrapping pliers to create a curve at the other end of the same piece of wire, making an S-curve (the larger portion of the S-curve will not be quite as rounded as the smaller portion) **(b)**.

3 Use a chasing hammer to hammer the piece. Avoid hammering the ends **(c)**.

4 Make a loop at each end in opposite directions **(d)**.

5 Using chainnose pliers, make an open spiral with a 3-in. (7.6cm) piece of wire to mirror the top curve of the S-curve component **(e)**.

6 When you're satisfied with the shape of the spiral, hammer it (do not hammer past the spiral) **(f)**. If it becomes slightly distorted, use chainnose and flatnose pliers to tweak it back into shape.

7 Trim the excess wire and make a loop at the end of the wire **(g)**.

8 String a pearl onto a headpin and attach it to the bottom loop of the S-curve component with a wrapped loop **(h)**.

9 Attach the S-curve-component and the spiral component with a pair of jump rings. Use a jump ring to connect the component to the earring wire **(i)**.

10 Make a second earring (change the orientation of both components to mirror the first earring).

Basics

a

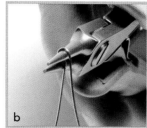
b

c

d

e

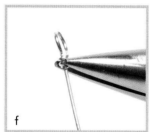
f

Wrapped Loop

1 Use the tips of chainnose pliers to hold a wire leaving a 3-in. (7.6cm) tail. Make a 90-degree bend over the pliers' jaw **(a)**.

2 Place roundnose pliers in the bend of the wire. Wrap the wire over the top jaw of the roundnose pliers until it touches the bottom jaw **(b)**.

3 Loosen your grip, rotate the pliers 90 degrees counter-clockwise (left-handers, rotate clockwise), and continue wrapping the loop around the bottom jaw of the round-nose pliers **(c)**. If the loop is not perfectly centered, use the roundnose pliers to center the loop. At this point, the wires should cross at a 90-degree angle.

4 Grasp the loop with chainnose pliers to stabelize it **(d)**. With your fingers or a second set of pliers, wrap the wire tail around the stem for 2½ or 3 wraps.

5 Trim the wire tail close to the wraps **(e)**.

6 Use chainnose pliers to tuck the wire end tightly be-tween the wraps. **(f)**.

Open a Jump Ring or Loop

1 To open a jump ring, use two sets of pli-ers to grasp the ring on each side of the opening. Use the tips of the pliers.

2 Move one set of pliers toward you and the other set away from you to open the ring slightly.

3 To close the ring, reverse the motion in step 2, until the ring is closed and there is no gap.

Use the same process to open and close a basic loop or the loop of an earring wire.

Knotting Between Beads

Use a needle or an awl to help position knots snug to the bead.

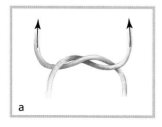
a

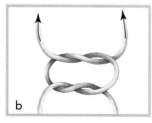
b

Square Knot

1 Cross one end of the thread over and under the other end. Pull both ends to tighten the first half of the knot **(a)**.

2 Cross the first end of the thread over and under the other end. Pull both ends to tighten the knot **(b)**.

Folded Crimp

1 String a crimp bead on flexible beading wire.

2 Pass the wire through the loop of the clasp (or other component) and back through the crimp tube.

3 Grasp the crimp tube in the back notch of crimping pliers. Be sure the wires are separate and not overlapping in the tube. Close the jaws tightly on the tube **(a)** so that each wire is enclosed in a channel created by the crimp.

4 Reposition the tube so it is in the front notches of the pliers. Rotate the tube so the indentation faces away from the pliers.

5 Close the jaws tightly so the tube folds in half, securing the beading wire **(b)**.

6 Trim the end of the beading wire close to where it exits the crimp tube **(c)**.

NOTE: Photos **d–g** show the crimping process with a double set of wires, as in the Dewdrop necklace on page 8.

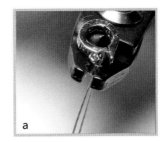
a

b

c

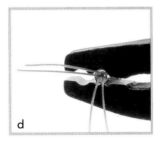
d

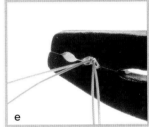
e

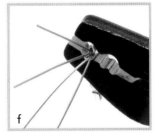
f

g

How to Add Patina

1 Dissolve a small piece of liver of sulfur in warm water and use tweezers to submerge the piece **(a)**. Periodically take it out to check the color.

2 Once you are satisfied with the color, rinse the piece in cold water, dry it, and use an abrasive pad to take off some of the patina, thus giving it contrast **(b)**.

a

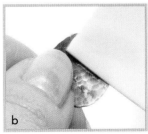
b

About the Author

Irina Miech is an artist, teacher, and author. She also oversees her two retail stores, *Eclectica* and *The Bead Studio*, in Brookfield, Wisconsin, where she teaches classes in beading, wirework, and metal clay. Her jewelry designs have been featured in *Bead&Button*, *Bead Style*, and *Art Jewelry* magazines. This is her eighth book with Kalmbach Publishing.

Other books by Irina Miech
- *Irina's Inspirations for Jewelry*
- *Metal Clay for Beaders*
- *Beautiful Wire Jewelry for Beaders 2*
- *Metal Clay Rings*
- *Beautiful Wire Jewelry for Beaders*
- *Inventive Metal Clay for Beaders*
- *More Metal Clay for Beaders*

Acknowledgments

I would like to thank my husband, Tony Miech, and my boys for their love and support.

Thank you to Lauren Walsh for her writing assistance. I would like to thank my editor, Karin

Van Voorhees, and the rest of the Kalmbach team for their invaluable assistance. Thanks also

to my wonderful store staff members for all of their enthusiastic help and continual support.

Explore more tips

from this talented artist

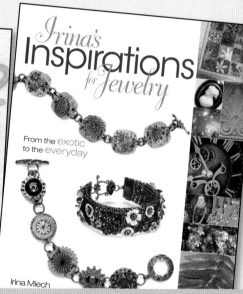